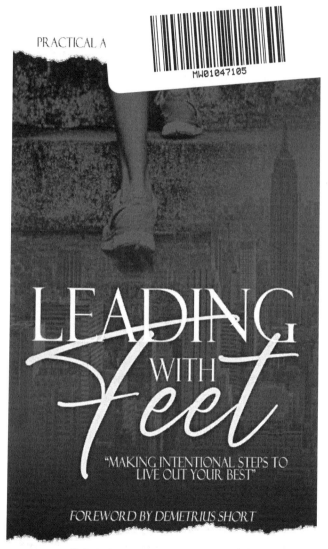

LEADING
WITH
feet

"MAKING INTENTIONAL STEPS TO LIVE OUT YOUR BEST"

FOREWORD BY DEMETRIUS SHORT

CHARELLE LANS

i

DEDICATION

So many times, in life, we take credit for things that can only be ordained by God. Things like vision, direction, and purpose are all facets of God's magnificent grace that covers our life. Recognizing that the concept for this book came during a low moment in life and seeing how the first version touched lives across the globe, it was only fitting to revisit this book and enormously expand on the concepts that were previously outlined.

This book is dedicated first to God. I honestly believe that when we focus on the things God has called us to do in life, we experience a multitude of expansion in every fiber of our being and our existence.

Secondly, to my son, nieces, nephew, family, mentees, supporters, etc., I am truly blessed to have you in my life, and your support means a great deal. This book is dedicated to every one of you.

To all those that choose to read this book and become inspired by the words that are contained within, there is so much purpose inside of you, and with the help of God, you can indeed manifest your dreams, visions, and legacy.

Believe in yourself. You are worth becoming who God has called you to be.

May we take this journey together? Life has so much more to offer than to just exist.

FOREWORD – Demetrius Short

"Every step you took was a step toward your success." – God

I was almost 18 years old in the early '90s walking three miles in between classes to my internships in a full suit, dress shoes, and carrying a briefcase. At the time, I had a goal to position myself for success, but I had an even bigger aspiration that I did not have a full grasp on yet. It started off so innocent with a goal to be the first of six siblings to graduate from college, but with no scholarship or transportation, quickly turned into an incredible journey with many forks, detours, and a whole lot of dead ends.

Where were my feet leading me? Your guess was as good as mine at the time. I occasionally found myself on campus with little food - sleeping between the dorm director's office and the couch of a friend. Despite reaching one of the lowest points in my life, I refused to stop moving, quit, and dropout! I deserved more than my name on a tombstone in the graveyard filled with college dropouts and unfulfilled dreams!

Years later, I returned to campus after completing my computer science degree, and nostalgically walked the same route I no longer had to travel. With tears in my eyes, I asked God, "Why did I have to go through this pain and struggle?" His response was, "Every step you took was a step toward your success."

It was at that moment; I developed a God-sized dream, hunger, and responsibility to help individuals and students overcome their own barriers in life to reach success and founded my non-profit, Transformation Life Center, where I vowed to run 3.1 miles in a full suit and sneakers in our annual Steps of Success 5K fundraiser.

Unbeknown to me, the past ten years, my feet would lead me to become a successful CEO of a thriving organization, leading a dedicated staff and thousands of runners and walkers with my feet to commemorate my struggle and inspire other's to never give up on their dreams.

My entire career has been a faith walk dedicated to pursuing the purpose of this must-read book you are about to experience and content you will easily digest, *Leading With Feet: "Making Intentional Steps to Live Out Your Best."*

So, I was honored and a bit shocked to be invited to write the foreword for this life-changing book. You see, less than six months ago, a divine, not chance, assignment allowed me to meet and share my story with award-winning, published author, Charelle Lans. We immediately became friends, and she shared her empowering wisdom with me. She is one of the most powerful, strategic thought leaders and transformational voices of today.

Hands down, she is one of the world's best-kept secrets! If you should have the pleasure of meeting her in person, you immediately experience how modest, humble, and bright she is. But as you get to know this "quiet storm" through the coming pages, you will find the journey of leadership her life has taken her on has uniquely qualified her to teach us about *Leading with Feet.*

Charelle has been an influencer in her professional career as a Segment Industrial Engineer for a multi-billion-dollar consumer products company where she has served as the Supply Lead for the largest Cat Care & Treats business in North America at the time. She is CEO of Vision Strategy Management, LLC business aimed at helping individuals and companies develop sustainable strategic success.

Charelle's revised book gives practical advice on developing the mentality necessary for the birth and execution of your goals. Is this book for you? Whether you are a business entrepreneur, college student, single mother, or professional in any capacity, this book teaches you the importance of creating movement to get things done!

Leading with Feet, "*Making Intentional Steps to Live Out Your Bes*" was written to inspire the stagnant individual that finds themselves saying: "I really want to, but..." and instills within the reader the belief that dreams, desires, and goals come alive when you make up your mind to take intentional steps towards them!

What I love about Charelle is she invests her "personal pains" she experienced along her journey and pursuit of her own pathway to success into practical advice and offered a wealth of proven practices to those who feel there's a bigger, more fulfilling life out there waiting for them. The next generation depends on you to take a step and get moving from fear to faith.

As you turn these pages, you will learn how to give yourself a PUSH past your fears and fuel yourself to make intentional, bold shifts to stop procrastinating and start flying to new heights! Every page will encourage and inspire you, like me, to become the person you were created to be.

As you read this book, you will learn how to create the space in your life to step out with intentional steps and align your actions to bring your dreams to fruition.

Wherever you are in the process and whatever state you may encounter, good or bad, this author leads you every step of the way, reminding you of the potential within you to create movement to achieve past, present, and future goals.

So, where are your feet leading you? Remember, the road nowhere will lead you somewhere. It is time for you to get off that road! Allow Charelle Lans's masterpiece, *Leading with Feet, "Making Intentional Steps to Live Out Your Best,"* the opportunity to help you divorce every negative momentum blocker in your mind, marry your heart and **take intentional steps** to navigate your life into a more profound, more prosperous and rewarding experience.

Prepare to live out your best life and impact the world. Prepare to Lead…with your feet!

Demetrius B. Short
Founder/CEO, Transformation Life Center, Inc., and Steps of Success 5k

PRELUDE

As a warm tear welled in the corner of her eye, blurring her vision, she silently collected her belongings from the security belt.

Refastening the black leather belt into her worn denim blue jeans, she felt a tear flow down her cheek and watched as it disappeared onto her black sweater.

As she bent down to put on her canvas slip-on shoes, she ignored the impatient passenger that was waiting behind her to gather their belongings.

Finally, with her shoes on, she watched yet another tear fall; this time, it splashed on the freshly buffed floors of the airport security terminal. Standing to grab her bag, she kept her eyes low while hopelessly wiping away the steady flow of tears that now streaked with traces of black mascara.

Hurriedly, she made her way to the nearest restroom.

"Keep it together, Sue."

She muttered to herself.

"Just keep it together."

Sue made her way to the dimly lit restroom and into the nearest stall. She flung the door to the stall open as the sound of the metal clasp hit the back of the plastic divider, allowing the noise to fill the quiet space.

Closing the door behind her with her back, she rested her head on the plastic door while gazing up at the ceiling. Her silent sobs now filled the air of the quiet restroom.

"Breathe, Sue," she told herself.

"It's going to be ok."

She encouraged herself, but the weight of the situation caused her to double over with grief. After a few minutes, Sue heard a knock on the door to the stall.

'Ma'am, are you alright?'

Bringing her mind back to the restroom stall and the reality of where she was, she peeked in between the stall doors to see a woman standing on the other side of the door.

"Yes, thank you."

Embarrassed, Sue wiped her tears in her sweater, unlocked the door and ran past the glaring eyes of the woman, and hurried out of the restroom towards her gate. Keeping her eyes low, she adjusted her book bag and walked through the airport.

"How am I going to get through this?" She thought. "This just feels so heavy."

She muttered to herself as the tears now visible flowed down her makeup smeared face. Her mind raced; she became lost in her thoughts and, for a moment, saw nothing but the weight of her eyelids.

"Fourteen years, two kids, and a career...gone" She shook her head while mumbling aloud to herself.

"If only there were something that I could do about it. Maybe I should see a counselor, or there's got to be a book or something I can read". She thought to herself.

As if her steps were divinely timed with her feet, she began to walk past a bookstore. It spoke to her. The ceiling to floor glass window radiated the show lights from within onto the terminal hall where she walked. She paused at the opening of the store and peered in.

"Wow, that looks really nice," she thought to herself.

In the center of the store stood an all-white and crystal book display case. Next to the case was a stand that read the words: 'Bestseller.'

The display case caught her attention and was so beautiful with rhinestones that lined the legs of the stand.

"I wonder what book will be placed there," she thought.

Sue was in the middle of a messy life transition and did not know how to reset.

In that split second, she felt somewhat hopeful. Yet as quickly as the hope came, it left as she heard the final boarding call for her flight departing Singapore.

She glanced at the open book display case once more and walked away as her thoughts returned to the reality of her situation.

Shoulders rounded while heaving slightly up and down as she cried.

Sue was devastated.

The Lesson of Sue

Sue forced me to write. Not only to write but to publish.

It was the visual depiction of Sue that brought me to taking the collective body of writings and publishing the first version of Leading with Feet, "Making Intentional Steps to Live Out Your Best."

Most mornings, my day is started in prayer and meditation. This particular day in my 4:30 am meditation; it was the visualization of Sue that brought me to tears. Sue needed something from me. Perhaps it was a learned experience, a shared revelation, or just an encouraging word.

She needed the very thing that I held hostage inside of me. She needed the very book that I was too afraid to write.

You see, what if the book that she would have seen on the shelf was the one that I was supposed to write? It was the vivid imagery of Sue not having the book that was locked away in me that awakened something within me.

It was the realization that the purpose of the journey was not meant only to be experienced by me but also to be shared with Sue and others, and that spoke to me.

So many times, we tell ourselves 'no' without ever giving someone else the opportunity to say 'yes.'

Too often do we silence our own voice and nullify the lessons of our journey because we think they are uniquely our own experiences, but the Sues of the world need you. They need you to share your lessons learned; they need you to share your story.

Someone, somewhere you may never get the opportunity to meet, may just need what you have to share. So, share it.

Imagine what could happen if we all chose to walk in our unique greatness and got out of our own way.

I invite you to lead with your feet. Act. Get out of your head and out of your way. Somewhere, someone needs what you have to share! So speak!

Charelle Lans

TAKING THE FIRST STEP

"One Decision Away"

I close my eyes and think for a while…
I see all my dreams manifested with God's grace and style...

I see people being transformed. I see inventions explored.

I see the newness of love and joy being restored…

All because I have chosen to embrace the intentions that God stored…

I close my eyes and see children smiling,

Their hearts filled with laughter.

I see men and women embracing their dreams and becoming all that God has called them to be.

I see young boys rising to the position of honorable men… growing and glowing.

I see them coming without end.

With my eyes still closed tight,
Life has a new meaning.

All because I chose to walk
In the fullness of my being.

Because I took a chance,

I stepped out on faith.
I danced in the rain on a stormy day.
I was happy inside to give it all and not hide
behind pride.

It was a good feeling to feel that I...

With my inventions, with my books, with my
gifting, could drive so much legacy and life!

As I opened my eyes, I realized that I could
have that life.
That my gifting did not have to stop just
because I woke up from my state of
daydreaming.

I did not have to be imprisoned to close-
mindedness, fear, or doubt

With all the light and life that can be given
held bottled up inside.

But my prayer, Dear Father, is to be fully content from within…
To leave what you have deposited in me into the hearts of men.

So, I wake up from my sleeping
I shake off idleness and stagnation.
I sit up, and I get up to awaken God's nation.

WE are gifted! WE are talented! WE are radiant and jubilant!

WE are awesome and powerful,

WE are truly exuberant.

Shake off the dirt!
Shake off the notion of hurt!

Get up and take a step knowing that YOU are blessed!

YOU are gifted!
YOU are made from God's hand.

YOU are the very being that He has called you to be.

If only, if only, you could open your eyes and see.

You can take the first step, and then another or two.
You can be everything and do what He has called you to do.

You are blessed! You are beautiful!

You are awesome! You are true!

You are the very change that you were waiting to be and do.

You can lead with your feet and take the first step.

You can live a life beyond your limitations.
You can be everything you could ever imagine or guess.

You do not have to take it to the grave.

You can leave your gifting to help the next generation. But the first step starts with you.
You must first be willing to step out on faith and choose.

So, what do you say?

The choice is up to you…
You are one decision away from the life you
were always due!

God bless you; I love you. I hope this book
inspires you.
I hope that you know that you are truly
bountiful.

Peace and blessings.

Charelle Lans

TABLE OF CONTENTS

Steps to Leading with Feet

INTRODUCTION

Often, we believe that our dreams are so far off in the distance that we have *time*. We convince ourselves that we can get started later because, let's face it, procrastination keeps us from being held accountable to the very thing that we value. Therefore, we talk ourselves out of taking the necessary steps that lead to intentional action. Yet, the concept of "having time" is quite comical if you think about it. It is an illusion of being able to reach into the future and 'order up' more 'time.'

Much like a woman giving birth, **all dreams/goals have due dates,** and the concept of "time" is just a social construct. "Time" is simply used to measure the distance between two points of reference. It was not intended to be a benchmark that governed action.

Recognizing that since time is an abstract measurement used to capture the spatial distance between moments or points of reference, it can be said that trying to control time is a waste of life and energy.

Honestly, one cannot control or manage something that was only designed to be measured.

The real question is: "What can you do with the moments of life, and how do you make your moments matter most?"

At times we've tricked ourselves into believing that we will always have the energy to get the essential things done, but the fact of the matter is we will not. Not always.

Energy is like currency.

You can waste it, save it, or invest it, and at some point, you will do all three. Where you attribute energy the most determines the extent of the impact you make. The real question is: '*Do you have the energy and fortitude to create an impact during the life of the opportunity?*' Grounding yourself around this fundamental principle can help propel you into immediate action rather than thinking that you will always have time.

Are you waiting to invest in your dreams because you feel the need will always exist?

Do you have nervous energy because you do not know what to expect, and the idea of actually 'making it happen' frightens you?

Regardless whichever is most prevalent for you:

A change in mentality is necessary for the birth and execution of a vision or dream.

Inactivity is, in fact, a choice. So why choose to stop before you even start? Why allow the dream to die inside of you? Why not move? All you need to do is breathe, relax, and be.

BEFORE THE FIRST STEP

Just after you have made up your mind, the leap of faith begins with the first step.

It has been said that dreams come alive when we 'wake up,' but what does that mean exactly? To 'wake up,' how and to what? Waking up physically either happens for you, or it does not. Even in the psychological sense, 'waking up' or becoming conscious of your dreams can occur, but does that really prompt you to act? Does the mere realization of your dream create the level of intentionality that is needed to inspire one into action? Perhaps not.

It is my belief that:

Dreams come alive when we make up our minds and take intentional steps towards them.

Not waiting for it to come to you but moving with active pursuit towards it, which requires energy.

Let us take the example of a boulder. It takes being intentional to move a boulder from its resting position.

It takes consistent energy, direction, determination, a little bit of strategy, and sheer tenacity, but once in motion, it will take out almost anything in its path.

Now, the analogy of a boulder is easy to conceptualize because we can physically see a boulder. It is a physical object, and we can envision it moving. It is a bit more challenging to expect movement for someone whose boulder cannot be seen with the natural eyes. It becomes more challenging to materialize a vision that cannot be seen or to find a way when there is no path, but when the direction is discovered, the potential is limitless for the individual. How much different is it for a stagnant individual who is inspired into action?

Leading with Feet, "Making Intentional Steps to Live Out Your Best" was written to inspire the stagnant individual that finds themselves making any of these statements:

"I would really like to begin my own my business, but…"

"I really want to pursue my dream, but I don't have the "time."

"I would love to move, but…"

This book is for you.

Leading with Feet, "Making Intentional Steps to Live Out Your Best," is about creating movement. It is about inspiring the ability to take tangible steps to bring your dreams, desires, and goals into existence.

Recognize that you must get moving because nothing happens until you can build momentum, and momentum cannot occur while we are stagnant. One must be in motion. So, let us get moving.

You are more than you may think you are.

You are more than your past, your fears, or even the perception of others; you were destined for greatness.

If you are ready, let us embark on this journey together to begin leading and living out our legacy. So, what are your feet leading you towards? What do you need to push out of the way to take that first step? If you are ready, let us get moving.

.

Chapter 1:

Gifts for the Grave

Moving from Fear to Faith

*"**The graveyard is the richest place on earth** because it is here that you will find all the hopes and dreams that were never fulfilled, the books that were never written, the songs that were never sung, the inventions that were never shared, the cures that were never discovered, all because someone was too afraid to take that first step, keep with the problem, or determined to carry out their dream."*

- Les Brown

Do not take your gifts or talents to the grave

Close your eyes and picture a cool dark place...

You cannot see or feel anything beyond the dampness of the space...

With your eyes still closed, envision the dream you always wanted to go after.

- - -

What does it feel like to achieve it?

How would your life change?

What emotions do you feel?

- - - -

Now open your eyes...
What if I told you that dark place was actually a grave?

...and the dreams you saw, were the life you were due

but did not quite achieve because you stopped short of the pursuit.

But why did you stop?

Or

Why didn't you start?

You see, your life is worth so much more,
Then just the mere beating of your heart.

Persist if you must,
But just don't quit.

Live on a deeper level

then to just exist.

You've got this!

The wonderful thing is
if you are reading this,

You can still manifest your goals
and live beyond the risks...

Charelle Lans

Moving from Fear to Faith

An integral part of 'giving yourself a push' is hinged upon our ability to shift our mindset by moving from 'fear to faith.'

*FEAR is an unpleasant, often **strong emotion** caused by expectation or awareness of danger.*
- **Miriam-Webster's Dictionary**

Miriam-Webster's Dictionary defined fear as a 'strong emotion,' not as an event, occurrence, or even an obstacle; but as a strong emotion. Yet this emotion is so strong that it stagnates our ability to excel. How is it that this one emotion could have so much power that it has the potential to alter our reality?

Why do we give fear so much control over our beings and authority over our lives? Why do we give something with such insignificance, so much value and weight? How can something that oftentimes not manifest keep us from moving into our destiny?

The artificial power of fear keeps one from manifesting dreams or realizing our potential. What is driving this fear? Is it one of these?

Fear of **success**: What if it does not work?

Fear of **failure**: What if it flops?

Fear of **self-insufficiency:** What if I can't?

Fear of **finger-pointing**: What will they say?

Fear of **finances**? What if it costs too much?

Fear of **false expectations**: What if it is not what I expect?

Fear of **challenge**: What if it's too hard?

Fear of **quitting**: What if I do not have it in me to finish?

Fear of **self-limiting beliefs**: What if I'm not good enough?

All these fears keep us from fully delving into the what-ifs of faith. What if we changed the what-ifs of fear to the what-ifs of faith? The same issues could have a vastly different outlook.

Faith for **success**: What if it does work?

Faith over **failure**: What if it flies?

Faith over **self-insufficiency:** What if I can?

Faith over **finger-pointing**: What can they say? Is it relevant, helpful, timely?

Faith over **finances**? What if I find the resources?

Faith over **false expectations**: What if it exceeds my expectations?

Faith over **challenge**: What if I can overcome it?

Faith over **quitting**: What if I find the drive to finish?

Faith over **self-limiting beliefs:** What if I am more than enough?

Perspective is fundamental

It is not until we are willing to move in faith and take the first step that we begin to manifest the things that are within us. Oftentimes, the things we fear do not manifest except in our own minds.

In fact, would you believe most of the preconceived reality of fear typically exists in one's mind?

While only a small percentage is manifested, we allow the smaller probability of fear to control the majority of what we do. Again, fear is a 'strong emotion,' but it does not have to become the reality that cripples our ability to succeed.

According to world-statistics.org, there are OVER 7.5 billion people on the planet; but only a few who control our most precious resources, invent lasting technology, or manifest their dreams. Where do you fall?

If you ask yourself what separates you from the world's pioneers, what you may find is it is often the 'what ifs' of our mindset.

If we are to live a thriving life, we must compress and eventually remove the control of fear that we allow to predominate our thoughts.

Tony Robbins challenged the mindset of getting this done with the following statement from his book, "Awaken the Giant Within" when he said,

"It's *not a lack of resources; it's your lack of resourcefulness.*"

- Tony Robbins

This statement speaks to the mindset that we have everything that we need to accomplish our goals, but what is really needed is a change of perspective.

As we transform our mental capacity, we find that we can have more success by carrying out our vision because the likelihood of fear pursuing or manifesting itself is slim.

In the same way, we selectively choose to focus on danger, doubt, and fear; we selectively and intentionally must decide to shift our thoughts to the things that strengthen our faith.

"Fear and worry are interest paid in advance on something you may never own."

- John Mason

The most considerable portion of activating one's gifting exist mentally, and it happens **before you take the first step** in an internal battle between fear and faith, but it does not end there. This battle exists on the continuum of life and is present even after you have taken several steps.

The battle also exists throughout your life as you raise the level of expectation and as you climb to new heights.

The only way to **overcome fear is by developing a greater level of faith**. A mental constraint such as fear can only be overcome by a deeper level of faith, stretching from one unknown to another. Fear cripples our ability to take calculated risks or steps towards our goals and holds us imprisoned to our thoughts.

Overcoming fear is necessary.

The more exposure we have to danger, the more we inherently become fearful... but in the same way that we assess fear, we should consider the risks of inaction. What is the danger of NOT moving? What happens if we don't shift?'. If we do not act, we inadvertently take our gifts to the grave.

So, how do you elevate yourself from fear to faith? How do you fuel yourself for the first step, create the mindset to move, or develop the discipline for destiny? How do you rob the graveyard of your dreams, visions, goals, ideas, or inventions?

"It takes intentionality and bold shifts..."

Chapter 2

GIVE YOURSELF A CHANCE.... PUSH

Chance implies that luck has something to do with success...The truth is that it requires action.

It takes intentionality and selective execution to give yourself a push.

Intentional and Selective Execution is taking deliberate action to shift your mind and create movement. When you move physically, your direction depicts your destination. Making sure where you are headed aligns with where you intend to go matters.

Making intentional and selective execution choices means that one must do so through the following means, which we will explore in greater detail:

Give Yourself a Push!

Strengthening one's faith sometimes requires a push to believe that you are powerful, capable, and able to obtain your goals. Stepping out on faith requires that you make up your mind; and to decide within yourself that it's worth going after, not stopping until you achieve it.

Get In Gear.... Get It Done!

Nothing is going change, transform, or manifest until you **physically** make it happen by converting potential energy into kinetic energy. A boulder is an example of this. It has potential energy stored within it until it is put in motion. In a resting position, the boulder is not threatening, but in motion, it can take out anything in its path.

"Faith without works is dead."

- James 2:20

Getting in gear is all about positioning yourself for success and to get it done through intentional and selective execution physically.

Give It Back or Give Ahead.... But Give!

Your legacy is weighty only when it can outlive you. When you can invest in others and give ahead, you are aiding to causes or missions that support others who face the same challenges you have overcome.

Recognizing that the next generation could be waiting on your ability to get in gear helps with the understanding that moving from fear to faith is not a choice, but action and responsibility that we are blessed to take. One's life is hugely successful when it gives life, offers learnings, and breathes legacy into others.

It Takes Intentionality and Bold Shifts.

As we explore Leading with Feet in greater detail, we will uncover exactly how to move into fulfilling legacy one step at a time...

Embarking Upon the Journey

"Before any battle begins physically, it first takes place mentally."

The first step is often the hardest because it is yielding to the unknown. Although you may have an idea of what is needed, and you may even speculate what you may need to do, but until you **actually do it**...you have not experienced what it feels like, and sometimes that's the scary part.

Taking the first step is the beginning of transitioning from having knowledge about something to gaining experience. But once the first step is taken, only then can you begin to assess the unique needs that are required to developing the stamina to endure. As you start to move, you may find that it is not as difficult as you thought it would be.

To make things happen, one would have to learn how to:

"Divorce their mind to marry their heart."

The heart is stored up with belief, with high hopes and dreams that are yet conceived. The heart holds the blueprint, and the 'make it happen somehow' attitude. The mind requires conditioning and renewal daily.

The mind is fixed on the perception of what things must be before they become.

Divorcing your mind to marry your heart means to keep developing an understanding with the mind to create the best possible outcome, despite limitations or preconceived realities that can be seen. Trade-in a short-sighted view for a long-term solution.

KEY EFFORTS BEFORE THE FIRST STEP

1. Visualize: Say it out loud before you can see it in view.

If you don't know your end goal, it becomes difficult to see just where you are headed.

"The self-demise mentality cripples the ability to succeed."

It also becomes hard to drive intentional steps in the area that you intend to go without becoming swayed by many distractions. Begin by mouthing out where you want to go daily. Defining your direction audibly is putting your desires into the atmosphere and creating intentional daily focus. This will be critical to determining the long-term direction.

Actioning your feet has a lot to do with clearly defining what you are working on or striving towards.

Start by identifying your 'big picture' vision. Where do you want to see yourself? What is your clear definition of 'success'? Answer these questions to set your direction:

1. What do I want to be remembered for in life?

2. What are my goals, and why are they important to me?

3. Why are my values vital to me?

4. What is something that brings me peace and joy that only I can do?

5. What are my unique gifts and strengths?

6. What can I contribute to the world as my legacy?

7. What is my purpose?

Start by looking at your aspirations.

As children, we believed that our dreams were often limitless! We think that we are invincible to danger, and we are fearless. Yet, as we get older, life, circumstance, and fear diminish the hopes of our youth. However, to walk out our aspirations, it is imperative that we relinquish our self-limiting beliefs that hinder our ability to visualize our future state. It is essential to have a vision of where you would like to end even before you start.

2. Quit the Self-Demise Mentality

Achieving long-term goals is like running marathons. They require overcoming mental barriers to reach your end goal.

I recall the mental struggles of running my first half marathon.

I was in the middle of a difficult chapter in life. I was in the middle of a divorce, and I desperately sought to control all the moving pieces of life, but it felt like the pieces were slipping through my fingers. I knew that I needed something to reinvigorate the very principles that I often helped others find clarity through. So, I decided to investigate doing a half marathon.

My end state was to develop personal stamina to withstand whatever trials I encountered during that difficult chapter in life. I began to envision what it would feel like to finish the race even before I started. I visualized myself dashing across the finish line with both fists in the air, sprinting across it.

This imagery was important to me because it helped me find a place of peace amid a situation that I felt went south.

Yet, the thought of accomplishing a half marathon when I had not so much as ran 3 miles seemed so out of reach. It excited, motivated, and intimidated me all at the same time.

What if I don't finish?'

The thought of not finishing the race, not having it in me, or not having enough endurance to finish frightened me. It Immobilized me and brought the flood of thoughts around my failed marriage back to the forefront of my mind.

What if I fail at this too?

What if I pass out?

What if I get injured?

What if I make a fool of myself?

What if I just do not have what it takes?

I was overwhelmed in the 'self-demise mentality. The mentality of failing before I had even given myself an opportunity to succeed. I was stuck in the battle of 'what ifs of fear.'

All those thoughts flooded my head and added to the negative thoughts I had about it before even walking one mile!

It is this very mindset that discourages many of us from even taking the first step. Furthermore, this self-demise mentality keeps us in the safe zone.

Just as these thoughts flooded into my mind giving me heart palpitations, I also experienced a flood of emotions that overcame my fears. It was the belief that I had too much to lose not to trust that **I could at least try.**

Ultimately, the absolute worse that could occur was that I do not finish the race, but if I did not at least try, then I would never know if it were something that I could complete. So eventually, I resorted to giving myself a push to get going.

3. *Get moving on your goals.*

The best way to get moving on your goal is to put one foot in front of the other. Sounds simple, right? Well, some things are just that simple, but we overcomplicate it. Just get started.

Often, I have tried to make elaborate plans that were extremely detailed. In my degree and training, I was taught to plan for every possibility of failure and then mitigate the issues. I would map out overly complex scenarios to balance out every 'what if' that could ever become the potential of reality. While having a concrete roadmap for execution is useful, especially important, and very necessary for strategic direction setting, you must remember to take it one step at a time.

Do not get stuck assessing every possibility that you obstruct the opportunity to perform.

After you have researched and assessed, sometimes you must just **get going on it**.

To do this, one must PAE the entryway...

Prepare, **A**ssess, and **E**xperience.

Preparation - Requires having vision and foresight in your heart even if it appears scary or uncertain. It requires taking the things that you already know "knowledge" and defining how to overcome the factors that can quickly become challenging deterrents.

It is doing the things that you know you need to do while preparing for the challenging opportunities; you set yourself up for planned success. Preparation considers doing the leg work in advance to understand the mental requirements of getting the goal completed.

Assessment - Requires taking an inventory to understand what your limitations are and developing an understanding of the areas that could become barriers. Conducting a thorough evaluation involves considering dynamic factors like timing, commitment, and training.

Assessing your capabilities offers insight into what your gaps and critical training opportunities are. The assessment also helps with having a view of potential distractions.

Experiences – This is where active learning takes place. This is the place where execution lives, and refinement occurs. This is where you begin to test your limits and develop a deeper understanding of what it feels like to be stretched.

The thing about getting experience is it requires that you learn along the way.

Some lessons cannot be taught on the sidelines. Some lessons must be taught in the game.

When you get in the game, you begin to know what it feels like to be slapped in the face, hit, or on the defense. From the bleachers or the sidelines, while you are preparing and assessing, you can observe that feeling, but there is a different kind of learning that takes place ONLY when you can get in the game and get hit.

To know what it feels like to sweat...is to understand what it feels like to develop character, tenacity, and persistence.

Surviving the experience to reach your goals takes the depth of character and persistence.

4. Persistence and Character Depth

*"Ambition is the path to success. Persistence is the vehicle you arrive in." - **Bill Bradley***

Goals and visions that are meaningful require persistence. Anytime you work on an idea or plan that requires other individuals, that vision or purpose requires patience and intentional pursuit.

People bring with them dynamics of how they think, operate, and assess the world in which they live.

It is essential to understand how to interact with people for the fulfillment of your goal. Secondly, if your goal is truly one that is a long-term sustainable change, then it will require having other people involved to ensure that it succeeds. This kind of goal is monumental.

The weight of a vision, goal, or dream can be either momentary or monumental. A fleeting goal is one that can be achieved with or without people and is accomplished within your lifetime. A massive goal is, in fact, a vision and typically requires the support and work of other people to support the execution of the goal.

5. *Getting in the game means stepping into the unknown.*

As you step into the unknown, you will begin to condition your heart and your spirit to develop the perspective of learning all the necessary tools for the successful execution of your goal.

Recognize that **learning occurs along the journey**; this helps to develop the stamina to sustain the tests of time. When you train for the race, you prepare for the obstacles that may come.

"Persistence can only be developed when you get wet and get hit."

Imagine that you are an athletic, open water swimmer. You may train for waves; however, when you get in the race, what you cannot prepare for is what it feels like to get hit in the face and how to respond to being hit. You can try very hard to mimic the conditions of the actual race, but there is just a different level of understanding that occurs by getting in and really experiencing what it feels like to execute.

This is important because when you say you are passionate about your goal and when you want to move in your plan, you must be willing to get in the water and not only survive but thrive amidst the highs and lows of the competition.

Persistence can only be developed along the way. Developing the fortitude to endure the race requires patience and training. Once in motion, you must awaken your senses. You must listen and understand what your innate response is to the conditions and be keenly aware of the circumstances that surround you.

Getting in motion requires adjustment and readjustment frequently. This gradual and continual tweaking refines your approach and perfects your ability to respond appropriately to the situation when it warrants a response. Always have a pad and pen, whether mentally or physically, ready to take notes and adjust your approach.

Be keenly aware of your internal response, constantly assessing 'why' These are key indicators of your natural response to challenging circumstances.

How fast is your heart beating?

What is your natural flow of thoughts?

Are they Positive? Negative? Optimistic? Pessimistic?

Do you encourage yourself to push through barriers or to stop working on your goals?

When you feel like giving up, do you remind yourself of why you started?

Assessing your thoughts and the external environment is critical to success in seeing it through.

Chapter 3

CALL TO ACTION

The best time of day is NOW. **- John Mason**

Are you spending each moment living on purpose?

The average life expectancy for a healthy individual in the US was roughly 78.9 in 2015- based on Data.worldbank.org.

If you do the math of where you are in life against this number, you may find that you have perhaps less than half a million hours left…

Every hour that passes is genuinely an hour less…

An hour less to give back, make an impact, write a story, tell a joke… leave a mark in history.

What are you doing each day to make your life, the lives of others, and the world in which we live better?

How is your existence adding value?

What are you doing to create your legacy?

Are you spending each moment living on purpose?

Lack of intentional action in the right direction is subjecting one's self to the impact of wherever inaction leads you, which often may not be where you want to go.

*Remember, every hour that passes is **an hour, more yet an hour less.***

Charelle Lans

THE BEST TIME TO START IS NOW!

It is my belief that there are two main reasons why people remain stagnant in their lives.

1. They either lack the confidence in their own personal ability to fulfill their goals, visions, and dreams.

OR

2. They overly prepare and get stuck in the repetitive cycle of "start, try, stop," "start, try, stop."

Both situations are detrimental to a person's confidence, and both conditions can lead to inactivity or a loss of passion and drive to fulfill their dream. The ironic thing about both cases is the constraint exists in the person's mind.

It is a belief system and a lack of follow-through that inhibits a person from genuinely pursuing their dreams in life.

"Master Your Mind...You Master Your Life."

This is not to say that you can and will not run into obstacles along the way; it simply means that you become what you believe you are to be. And when I say belief, I truly mean what you physically execute each day. While someone can idolize becoming healthy:

A true belief governs your actions.

A belief prompts action and creates a core sense of accountability.

Recognize there is no greater time to start working on your dreams than the present.

Life exists in the present, and as we work out our dreams, we must become more diligent about pulling our thoughts into our current reality that dictates action.

Whenever we have a list of tasks, we call them an action list or an action item. There is no coincidence the first word on that list is 'action' which requires movement from the place of inactivity. The list is not called a thought list, and while thought lists are important, they do not require movement.

Whereas an action list requires that you 'do something' to get your goals accomplished. Sometimes, it takes commitment and courage to move.

It took me a long time to begin to understand what it meant to get my feet in motion. It was not until I hit that rough patch in life that I began to step out on faith. I tried to bring what felt like an inconceivable vision into actionable steps that I could take in the current.

> It was the end of 2011, and I was at a very vulnerable time in my life. I was on the verge of a divorce, drowning in medical bills with a sick toddler, and desperately trying to manage being a 'put together mom' for my son, while balancing my career and sanity.

I was overwhelmed with so many life changes hitting me all at once. Up to that point, I had what I thought was a sound way of managing stress, but this time it was different.

So many challenges all at once, it was hard to see the light at the end of the tunnel.

There must be a better way, if I could just find a better way, I thought to myself.

You see, for the first time in my life, I was challenged with the decision of choosing fear or faith. I could let the fear of not rebounding to overcome me and become immobile and stagnant, or I could have faith. I recognized that while I was unable to see a way out at that moment, having a belief that there would eventually be a way through the situation kept me going.

I needed something to take my mind off it. Something that could shift my focus in a way that added positive momentum back into my life, and I began to play with the idea of doing my first half marathon.

I recall my whole mental uncertainty associated with wanting to get started with the half marathon.

Thirteen miles! Wow, that is a long time and a long way. Why would someone want to run that far without being chased? Nope, not going to happen!

I dismissed the thought from my mind only to revisit the idea a few days later. This time, my approach to doing it was more inquisitive.

hew… can I really handle 13.1 miles? I mean, who does that anyway?

You see, at the time, I was not running at all, and although I ran competitively in high school, it was only for short distances. Long-distance was not an interest of mine until this time, and it was only because of my situation.

Nevertheless, my curiosity about learning more about it drove me to take some initial action.

I began to research half marathons and look at pictures of people running. I began to experience the emotional connection to seeing various causes and money being raised for individuals and charities alike. It was this emotional connection that increased my interest in doing a race, yet I still battled with the physical reality of doing one.

Hmmm, I thought. *I wonder what it feels like, probably hurts, but even if I wanted to do it, when would I find the time? Who would watch my son? Nope, even if I really wanted to do it, it just seems impossible.*

I dismissed the thought of running my first half marathon for the second time as 'impossible.'

The third time I revisited the thought was when I came across a race in Orlando, Florida, through a very well-known theme park.

Hmmm, this looks interesting.

I began to research the race, looked at the pictures, felt the connection, and began to envision myself in the race.

This is one that could be done with friends. It seems like it is not a 'race,' but a long fun run.

I wonder what it would be like to finish a race like this. Maybe I will just get on the treadmill and see how I feel.

I got dressed, put on the first pair of shoes I could find, and just started walking. After a couple of minutes, I began to feel fatigued. I became winded and felt my muscles begin to ache.

Whoo! This is harder than I thought. I looked down at the distance screen, only a quarter of a mile!

Wow! I have a long way to go if I want to get to 13.1 miles. Can I really do this? I challenged myself.

I wasn't ready to fully commit; I needed more evidence that I could do it.

I spent the next few days going back through this cycle of research, connection, doubt, possibility, slow start on the treadmill, then back to research... until one day, I finally decided regarding the race. I wanted to believe that I could do it. I wanted to believe that it was possible. I was ready to stop doubting and decided to give it a try.

What is the worst that could happen? I can always quit.

I started with the worst possible thought of accepting defeat before I had even begun, but it was enough to get me to commit. Although I made some progress in my commitment process of doing a half marathon, I was still plagued with the self-demise mentality.

Sometimes, we must prove our way through our own limitations to find a deeper belief in our own capabilities. Sometimes it takes proving your way through to get to a stronger belief of 'what if I succeed.

I picked what I thought was the right race, and I gave myself six months to train. I registered and paid for the race.

Ok. I am committed. Whether I am ready or not, the race is coming in six months.

This forced me into action. The suggestion that 'ready or not the race was coming' propelled me to get moving, and it gave me a positive milestone to look forward to during turbulent times.

My first race was a direct reflection of my belief in my ability to overcome emotional pain. I figured that if I could overcome 13.1 miles, then I could get through a rough chapter of my life. For me, this half marathon was more than just a race; it was

A physical representation of an emotional and mental struggle.

The first few weeks were a real challenge. I remember going back and forth in my mind thinking about the fact that I did not have any time to train. In fact, I did not engage in a lot of training at first. Instead, for me, it was **figuring out what needed to change in my life**.

At first, it seemed impossible, but then I became more intentional, strategic, and creative.

I decided I would just place one foot in front of the other, and then do it repeatedly.

And that is just what I did. I took it one step at a time, picked a park, and started to walk.

What I learned in doing that was I found space in my life. I started to get up earlier, walk during my lunch, or leave earlier. I eventually got to the place of taking my son along for the ride in his stroller for my Saturday morning 5ks.

Before long, my walks became therapy for me. It gave me a moment to figure out how to balance out life. I also learned during that time; **I found the time I thought I did not have.**

That season of my life was extremely difficult yet rewarding. I learned about different techniques, got the training plans, training buddies, and ultimately it became a race for a better life for me. It all started with my ability to recognize the need just to move, get started, and get going.

Chapter 4

GIVE UP without GIVING UP

*The most important decision about your goals is not what you are willing to do to achieve them, but **what you are willing to give up.***

- Dave Ramsey

To pursue your dreams, you must give up something. If your goal is to lose weight, giving up junk food is necessary...if your goal is to run a race, giving up lying around the house for training is necessary. If your goal is to establish a business, you must give up scrolling on social media or any other habit that prohibits you from accomplishing your goal.

Destruction is always necessary before construction.

The land must be cleared out before new seeds can be planted. The process of clearing helps the crop to grow. The same can be true when you are aspiring to pursue your dreams. Something should be given up or supplemented with your new way of being.

Problems arise when we attempt to keep old habits that are in direct conflict with our goals. We trick ourselves into thinking that both can be achieved, but:

Commitment is not and does not exist in the gray.

A commitment either is, or it is not. The same can be said about what must be given up to pursue your goal.

Operating in the gray only delays the time in between your start and expected finish.

GET IN GEAR TO GET IT DONE

"Success is like a snowball…You have to get it going, and the more you roll it in the right direction, the greater it gets."

*- **Steve Ferrante***

Start Where You Are

"The longer we take to act on an idea, the more unclear it becomes. Procrastination is a choice that holds us back and makes us miss the best opportunities."

– John Mason

One of the biggest misconceptions about why we do not achieve our dreams is the belief that we do not have the money, time, or resources to get started. This could not be farther from the truth. In fact, we have everything that we need to transform our lives.

Sometimes its research, sometimes it is finding the right mentor, or sometimes it is writing out a simple, disciplined plan. A piece of paper and a pen can go far in defining your goal.

In starting where you are, you assess all the resources in front of you and become creative, inventive, and a crusader in your own mission. You naturally become gifted in finding the perfect solution for creating the path you want to carve for your life.

When you start where you are, you begin to develop the **muscle memory** needed for replicating success, and once you begin, it is inevitable that you will become better over time.

As you critique your craft or master your skill, you become more effective in defining the appropriate actions that need to take place.

Do not become caught into the cycle of believing you do not have what you need to get started and remain stagnant.

All you need to do is get moving.

As you begin to get moving, you will discover the necessary steps that are needed to establish your path.

Recognize that your plan does not need to be perfect for you to get started. You will learn along the way. Every step takes intentionality and movement.

The Process of Movement

Execution requires movement. Once you have convinced yourself to move, the next step is just to do it. However, some things are easier said than done.

It takes discipline, desire, drive, direction, and intentional decision making to progress through the continuum of building the momentum that creates movement. While we would love to think that the continuum is linear, it is actually an oscillating cycle weaving back and forth between the phases of starting and stopping until you get to the place of rest.

This respective field of pushing and pulling helps to build character depth and the necessary skill sets to achieving goals and dreams in life.

When a child learns to walk and falls down 50 times, he never thinks to himself: "maybe this isn't for me?"

- Steve Mehr

Even before we were born, our parents were always taught that movement was a good indication of growth. Doctors would measure the success of a pregnancy based on how a fetus grows throughout the gestational cycle. Even after birth, one way that the development of the child was measured was based on ensuring the baby has the proper level of movement and weight. Movement is, therefore, necessary for growth, development, and ultimately success.

As a parent, I remember when my son was an infant, learning how to move. There he lay on the bed on his stomach with his little legs wiggling in the air. He could barely hold his head up. He made noises such as little coos and groans of his personal satisfaction; and wiggling his body but getting nowhere. Just watching him looked more like he was swimming in the sheets.

As a parent, I would get so excited to see him wiggle and roll on the bed; rocking his body from left to right.

Just like a fan in the stands, I cheered him on, "Alright, man, you can do it!"

With a warm smile, I was delighted to see him squirm. His squirming and movement were indications that he was becoming more and more comfortable with his limbs. The more comfortable he became, the more confident he moved. He figured out that he could squirm and scoot his way from one side of the bed to the next successfully without help. In his preliminary moments of movement, he discovered use for his body.

When we think about the process of creating movement, its essential to return to the fundamental stages of child development. 'How can the process of movement be defined based on the development stages of a child, one may ask? Or why would we even consider it?

Lessons can be uncovered in the simplest occurrences of life. In fact, the principles of life are evident in the early stages of life, and as we grow and mature, sometimes, it becomes imperative that we return to these basic truths. So, as we explore the process of movement, consider the movement milestones of a child.

The process of creating movement can, therefore, be broken down into four basic steps:

Creeping→ Crawling→ Walking→ Running

Chapter 5

Creeping→ Crawling→ Walking→ Running

The first step in the physical process of creating momentum is all about getting started. As we elaborate on this, consider a child.

CREEPING: Wiggle Where You Are

The primary step considered **Creeping** is consistent with what you see with babies when they begin wiggling and moving their body to get going. They begin to wiggle their body and get into a tempo or rhythm that helps them to create movement through discovery. Discovery in the stage is what we are after.

At that point, having clarity on the steps to move in an intended direction is not the focus and is irrelevant. The main purpose is to **move and discover the functionality** of their limbs as they explore use for their body.

The same can be said of an individual at the beginning stage of striving towards a new goal. In the first phase of Creeping, we define what we can do. Simply put, start moving!

When we start moving towards a goal, it may feel a bit awkward at first and perhaps unorthodox but keep moving! At this stage, conditioning the mind is an imperative first step. Secondly, having the mindset to get moving is critical. Third, at this stage, knowing exactly how everything will come together is less critical than knowing where you would like to end up. We may not have all the pieces, we don't know exactly how we are going to achieve our goal, but we do know that we have somewhere we need to be.

The more comfortable we get with moving, the more likely we are to build momentum, and momentum is exactly what we are after. The first characteristic of moving is recognizing the simple fact that you can. You can, at any moment, decide to move.

Energy is invested upfront as one comes to know their ability to move and establish direction. Just like a child learning to move, it is a slow and gradual start. Mistakes made at this stage are less costly, and is, therefore, easier to shift directions at the beginning of a new goal.

Scooting/Creeping is just the beginning. As evolution through self-discovery occurs, refining your direction is necessary to accomplish your goals more efficiently. It is, however, necessary to accomplish creeping before you can move to the next phase.

CRAWLING: Work What You Have

The second step in this process is building effectiveness. We will refer to this as *crawling* in the same way that a baby crawl. The motions of crawling help a child get from one side of the room to the other with **stability and direction**. The key aspect of this phase is: stability and direction.

They have mastered creeping, the phase of discovery, and can now move more comfortably in the direction of their choice. Although it is not yet the most efficient way to move, it is a more effective means of getting around than creeping.

As you consider your goals, consider crawling. Once movement has been created through creeping (discovery), refinement through building effectiveness follows. Effectiveness must be both stable in an intended direction.

Effectiveness builds consistency towards goals. It positions the individual on a path of preservation and builds momentum.

Consider this: You have started to work on your goals, and now you get into the cycle of start/stop. You know what you need to do, where you aspire to be and are working to build consistency.

This is the cycle of 'Start -Try - Stop' and mistake making continues in this step. As you build effectiveness, taking personal inventory of gaps and opportunities is important in the fulfillment of building effectiveness. As you become agile in this phase, refinement and muscle memory also begin to occur.

Crawling is a necessary step before you can walk or run. Clarifying your direction, building momentum, and refining your vision typically occurs in this step as well.

WALKING: Moving with Meaning

The third step in the process is building efficiency. Once you have started to move through Creeping (discovery), and you have built effectiveness through Crawling (stability & direction), the next step is to create efficiency through Walking (discipline).

As a child transitions from Crawling to Walking, they fall consistently, and although painful at times, it is necessary for their motor development skills. Creating efficiency works to build consistency in the same manner.

It is through the steps of learning to transition between Crawling to Walking that one will face some degree of 'opportunity' that will challenge the level of commitment to continuing in their goal.

This is where self-discipline is essential to building efficiency. Discipline creates dedication and commitment to the goal even when mistakes are made.

The key is to keep working at it and moving through it regardless of how it feels. This step of building efficiency not only cultivates discipline but refines accuracy.

Every step builds muscle memory towards the pursuit of your goals, and sometimes regression is necessary for progression. Each step builds cadence, consistency, confidence... When you walk, you are, in fact building your stamina to achieve your goals.

RUNNING: Leading with Speed

The fourth step in this process is when mastery of the preliminary steps has occurred, and you can now transition to running. This is a step where we oftentimes want to arrive too soon, but we must take the necessary steps to get here.

Running (drive) is where we began to do what we do best, and we begin to learn how to replicate success. We have done the work to discover, build effectiveness, efficiency, and now we can execute with diligence and speed in the appropriate direction.

This is the component that ladders up to us, achieving our goals.

While this step is oftentimes, the one that we aspire to achieve quickly, it is the step that is not possible without having gone through the process of the previous steps.

Stamina to endure difficulties, muscle memory to replicate success, determination to see it through are all fundamental in the phase of running, and the same is true for one's ability to pursue their goals.

Each step that you take is necessary for providing gradual improvement, building your strength, endurance, and your character as you progress through each step. As you grow, each step becomes easier than the last, hence the momentum that builds as you continue to expand. The same can be true when you think about your goals, dreams, and destiny.

Muscle Memory

Muscle Memory Leads to Mastery

At the start of anything new is habit building. The grunt work to establish disciplined habits that carry you through the rest of the journey. Often, starting a new habit is much easier than sustaining it. The latter comes only with intentional focus, rigor, and energy to overcome the initial feelings of 'wanting to quit.'

Getting started takes time. It takes diligence and consistency, much like a baby learning to scoot. It is a bit awkward. You start, then you stop, you put it down, come back to it, and then start over again...It's this awkward process of starting and stopping that makes it hard to build momentum and muscle memory at first.

Just know that:

This is all normal.

As you get better, strengthen yourself, and focus on where you are attempting to go, you become more effective. This state of effectiveness comes with repetition, and repetition is what helps to build muscle memory.

Muscle memory is a term that is commonly used in sports as a form of conditioning that trains your brain to repeat an action consistently. A basketball player practicing the same shot repetitively is a good analogy of creating muscle memory.

The same holds true for new habits; ultimately, we want to train our brain into habitual behaviors. Whatever your desired goal is, do something towards it DAILY.

If your ambition is to become a great athlete, practice your sport. If you want to become a better swimmer, practice swimming often. If you want to become a better decision-maker? Make more decisions!

The old saying:" Practice makes perfect," If I were to paraphrase, I would say...

" Practice makes muscle memory, and muscle memory makes perfect."

The more discipline that you build into doing what you already know to do, the more effective you will become in it.

If you are starting something new, seek out resources to help you fine-tune your craft. Seek out others that are already talented in what you are attempting to do. These individuals can help with preparation, lessons learned and being accountability partners in the fulfillment of your goals.

Getting to the next level requires building muscles that you may not be accustomed to using in order to grow.

As with any physical muscle growth exercise, recognize that it will likely require some level of discomfort. As you grow from one level to the next, getting accustomed to being *strategically* uncomfortable, asking for help, seeking out resources, and staying focused to get it all done becomes increasingly important.

These actions help to build discipline, and discipline overtime builds muscle memory, which leads to mastery.

Emotional Connection

Emotional Tie or Connection

Emotions are powerful. As explored earlier, emotions can be so strong that they stagnate, like we discussed concerning fear. However, equally as important, emotions can help to compel a person into action. It is typically using our emotions that we develop meaningful connections and base the initial decisions to engage.

Having an emotional tie to your goal or vision is essential to its success. Emotional ties can be based on an internal feeling to an external event or activity. An emotional tie is a driving force that connects you to your goal stimulated by either past occurrences or future aspirations.

Emotional ties ground you to your goal and make the decision to pursue them relevant. In order to remain committed to any goal that you are striving for, you must have the foresight to envision yourself obtaining it and the ability to relate it back to something.

Envisioning success in obtaining your weight loss goal, fitness goal, or any other goal you desire is important to solidifying the objective in your mind.

When I decided to run my first half marathon, I started with my desired end state in mind. I began with envisioning myself crossing the finish line with my hands clenched into tight fists acknowledging that I had accomplished such a feat that I set out to do. I imagined myself expressing a deep sigh in satisfaction and a stream of flowing tears of joy and having finished a journey that felt insurmountable at first.

The more I envisioned seeing myself at the finish line, the more I desired to get through to it, resolved to fight for it, and see it through.

This was the first emotional tie that I created for doing the race.

The second emotional tie that I had with my half marathon was being able to race alongside people who were doing the exact same thing who believed that, although it did not seem possible at the start, we were all determined to see it through.

Having a personal connection to your goal, and the ability to see **a greater synergy that it creates with others helps** to ground you to your goal. It keeps you centered on finishing it regardless of the circumstances that surround you.

As you are working on manifesting your vision/ goal, there will be unplanned circumstances to arise, which will challenge your commitment. However, if you have an anchor to your goal, you can push and press through it.

I remember the moment that I was faced with the decision to continue or to stop and quit.

I was rounding mile four on my race, and up until that point, the race was flawless! The support from the fans was amazing; people were cheering at every turn.

"You've got this!" "Keep going!" they shouted.

The adrenaline kept me pushing. It was as though I was floating on cloud nine. Music pumping in my ears while snapping to the rhythm of the beat. The many days of preparation and planning were paying off. My mood matched the momentum of the crowd; energetic, optimistic, and hopeful.

Then came a bend in the course that took the race through a quiet drive through the closed theme park.

At about 5 am in the morning, the sun was not yet up, and apart from the panting sounds of runners through the park, it was relatively quiet. As if timed perfectly, with the environment, I began to feel excruciating pain in my right knee.

A pain that I became all too familiar with as part of my training. It was the kind of pain that felt as if someone was driving a knife through my knee, sharp and stabbing. At first, I ignored it. I thought to myself,

> *'If I don't acknowledge it, maybe it will eventually go away.'*

This was a lesson that I too quickly came to learn on the course. Sometimes, you cannot just barrel through your journey and not acknowledge the necessary changes that beckon your attention along the way. Secondly, when faced with an unexpected obstacle, pretending that the issue does not exist does not resolve the issue. It only gives it more time to fester and grow or get worse. Stop and address it! In my case, it got worse, nevertheless, back to the story.

So, I pushed through and kept going; only the pain did not go away. Having experienced a similar issue in my training, I recalled having to sit out a whole month because I did not properly aide to my knee. I pulled back to a slow stride and then down to walking for a bit. Up until that point, my thoughts were positive towards completing it, and for the first time in the race, all the doubt about finishing the half marathon returned.

I looked around to see if there was a place to stop and band my knee and determined it was too dark to stop and according to the course outline, the next medic was at the halfway mark.

'Just perfect,' I thought.

On my race outfit, I wore a pin. It was the exact replica of the finisher's medal. I took the pin off my clothing and examined it.

Tears began to well in my eyes as the idea of quitting the race began to dominate my thoughts. I contemplated what it would mean in the bigger context of why I was doing the race in the first place. The pressure felt too heavy.

For a moment, I let the feeling of defeat overtake me. I continued to walk, and with music in my ear, I kept moving. With the pain still eminent, I stretched at every chance that I got, but I kept moving. Amid my spiral of doubtful thoughts, **I kept moving.**

In the quiet moments of life, while you are working on your goals, there will be times when the

'peril feels greater than the possibility.'

Do not be overcome by it. Chart your course, and stay focused on your goal. Take an inventory of yourself, stop and readjust if you must, but stay the course and keep going. If you find yourself overcome with mental stagnation, get moving. Sometimes, you must keep 'physically moving' until your thoughts catch up.

As my breathing returned to normal, I began to realign my steps to the tempo of the music. Although the tears still flowed, I clenched onto the miniature pin and just continued to walk.

I saw a sign just up ahead, and it read 'Mile 5'. At that moment, I realized that although I was in some pain, that I had made some progress. Still less than halfway, but:

Halfway were only a few steps away.

When we find ourselves in the 'bend' of our goal where it seems impossible to achieve. Set your sights on smaller, more manageable milestones that lead you to the long-term aspiration. In doing so, progress is more measurable, and accomplishing the smaller milestones help to refuel the desire to complete it.

It felt like halfway would never come, but I repeated it to myself over and over with each step. I began to refocus on my breathing and the music.

Another sign just up ahead, 'Mile 6'. "Halfway IS only a few steps away!" I was hopeful.

I began to shift my thoughts back to the race; the sun was coming up. The thoughts of finishing the race reemerged as I thought about crossing the finish line,

'I can do this.'

I began to think of others who could push through to come out victorious, and I resolved that would be my story too. I began to focus on my breathing and to synchronize my breathing with my steps.

'I can do this! All I have to do is keep moving, and eventually, I will get there.' *One step at a time.*

I began to see the crowds again, and hear the excitement, felt it too. After a stop to the medical tent to examine and band my knee, I resolved to finish the race. It meant too much to me not to.

There will be times when you hit barriers along the way, and while I would not advise injuring yourself to finish a race, you must be willing to make the best strategic decision for yourself.

Having a deep connection with your goal is necessary for finishing the race.

Too often do we not know why we want to accomplish the things we want to go after. As a result, we do not develop a frame of reference for a deeper connection as to why we want to do something.

Therefore, we become shoppers of *incomplete good ideas*. Understanding the goals we have is extremely important and keeping the goals in perspective helps us to achieve them.

There are various levels to increasing your emotional tie with your goal, which starts with a desire. As you work through the process of building momentum, this emotional tie strengthens, and this desire turns to discipline.

The bond between desire and discipline is deep but can only grow where there is dedication.

Without an emotional connection internally, it is difficult to reach your goal when times become tight, and stakes get high.

From the perspective of an external connection, every goal or vision that you have is bigger than yourself. While it is nice to do things that feed the ego, creating lasting change and lasting fulfillment is necessary to develop a connection that is external to your being. This could be proven by connecting to a larger organization where you are able to contribute your goals/visions/talents or writing a book to help others.

Developing a business idea that either employs others or provides a service could very well be developing a platform.

The point is that the options are endless. Whatever you decide, having an emotional tie that is external helps to create generational growth beyond yourself for years to come.

When you say that your goal or your vision is connected to a bigger or broader picture, then you can sustain change.

The external connection is needed to sustain the vision, create lasting impact, or pioneer legacy. Whenever you are working or building momentum towards something, think about ways in which it can be connected to a larger and broader audience than just doing something for solely yourself.

The second can be a bit more challenging and scarier because it requires layers and levels of humility as well as involving other people in your vision. Recognize that we are part of an interconnected network where we all balance each other out and work together.

"Human behavior flows from three main sources: desire, emotion, and knowledge."

- Plato

Accountability

Accountability

"The moment you accept responsibility for everything in your life is the moment you can change anything in your life."

- Hal Elrod

There are two layers of accountability that must be taken into consideration when pursuing your goals. The first one has to do with personal accountability. This simply implies that

"I am responsible for the actions that I take or inactions that I choose to make."

Accountability beckons action. By holding oneself accountable to the fulfillment of goals are essential to bringing them into view.

Personal accountability acts as a mirror and allows you to reflect on what you want to see. Asking yourself the tough questions like:

What are my goals, and why are they important to me?

What is the result that I am seeking to obtain?

What do I need to move out of the way?

When do I start?

When do I finish?

What do I measure?

How do I know if I am successful?

Who should I include along the journey?

Who will be impacted because of what I am doing?

How will I create a process that will sustain?

Asking yourself tough questions, and holding yourself accountable to answering them keeps your goals at the top of your mind. There is nothing that says accountability quite like writing things down and making it measurable.

Having a mental and physical measurement of some sort that defines when the end or start is creating clarity for your goal.

Whether it is a goal or vision that you are attempting to achieve is one thing, and the other thing is to have an accountability buddy or someone that holds you accountable for obtaining your goal.

Having someone who is willing to push you like a coach can help you reach your goals. The second layer of accountability that is necessary is keeping your goals as a necessity. The accountability person's job is to keep your goal at the forefront of your mind and to challenge you so that it does not become obsolete.

An accountability partner takes the goal that you have written down, put up somewhere, and allocated time to keep it a part of your cognitive mind, your conscious mind.

Your accountability partner is constantly reminding you that your goal is vital in this stage so that you are actively working towards it, and if not, to help you readjust when necessary.

Accountability buddies are incredibly important when it comes to moving into your vision, goal, and purpose.

Chapter 6

GIVE IT BACK

At the last lap of the race, the crowds were on their feet, cheering. The energy was contagious! I was limping, but still standing. Still pushing. My legs felt like spaghetti, but at least I felt them.

Beads of sweat poured down my face mixed with some level of tears. The closer I got to the finish line, the more I reflected on the journey. It was tough, painful; I fought quitting, but I was about to finish. I started to smile widely!

WOW! This is really about to happen, I thought, and then it happened...

I did it!

My family was there, and we all cheered! With a shout of satisfaction coupled with tears, I bent to accept the adorning of my medal.

The metal symbolized **a new physical representation of the mental and emotional struggles that I endured.**

I did it!

It was at that moment I realized that I could accomplish anything I set my mind to accomplish. I also recognized that the steps to getting to that place was not straight and easy, but required persistence, tenacity, and fortitude to move and keep my feet in motion.

This race was a symbolic representation of getting through a difficult patch in life. The application of being able to overcome a mentally daunting obstacle (in this case, a divorce) by associating it with a physical challenge (in this case, a race).

It's easy to see and believe tangible things exist because you can physically see it. It is more difficult to see an intangible thing (such as your goal or a vision) because you cannot physically see with the natural eye when you conceive it.

Yet, if you are able to associate your goal or vision with taking on a physical challenge (race, a new sport, painting, etc.), the learnings related to overcoming the self-demise mentality and other internal battles become transferable.

Before long, you will be operating in your success.

There will be times when you falter, fall off course, and experience setbacks, but know that you can always get back on track. Also, know that even when you get to the place where you are running, you're running with a baton, and you must pass along the information that you learned to the next generation before you return down to walking, and finally resting.

Once you have gotten the motion going, keep the motion going.

Batons are passed in motion, not while standing still.

Give something back. Give your time to teaching resources. Help the next person to pick up where you left off and grow from what you know.

We should be able to continue to build upon what has already been put in place rather than go backward.

It is up to us to help others identify how to bridge the gap from Creeping➔ Crawling➔ Walking➔ Running. It is a process that must take place.

Ralph Waldo Emerson said,

"Do not go where the path may lead. Go instead, where there is no path and leave a trail."

Leave a trail long enough that when the next generation sets it ablaze, it will light up the entire world.

Create blocks that are solid enough to build onto from one generation to te next. Live beyond your years, but to get to this place, you have to get started right now, right where you are. Be mindful of the pitfalls, and get started.

Chapter 7

GET OUT OF THE PIT...

On the Brink of Greatness

On the brink of greatness is a steep and narrow cliff…

Accomplishing great works and setting the trail ablaze is great when it comes to discovery…

*But if one is not careful, they may find themselves only **a few steps shy of a long fall.***

Arrogance typically assumes its place in the face of greatness.

It is easy to become consumed in the hype.

Instead of getting too caught up, simply remember what it took to arrive at that place, take a deep breath, and know that there is still more to accomplish.

For the work of someone that is genuinely great does not just stop with what is done only 'today.'

The minute you believe that you have "arrived" will be the exact moment that you stop growing and take one step closer to that fall.

Stay humble.

Keep your eyes open, and your mind focused. There is more work to be done.

Charelle Lans

Common Pitfalls

When striving to accomplish your goals, be mindful of the common pitfalls that can stagnate your growth and ability to accomplish your goals. Let's explore a few of them below.

Common Pitfalls are:

1. Taking on too much too soon

2. Failing to Plan Effectively

3. Not having a precise measure of intentionality

4. Wishing without Working

5. Becoming distracted by 'Naysayers'

6. Expecting Perfection on the first try

1. Taking on too much too soon

Conditioning yourself for the journey to ensure success is an important step. Creating time to build the infrastructure to sustain your goal is equally as important.

Give yourself time to build muscle memory to ensure repetitious success. For example, running a half marathon for the first time requires practice, intentionality, research, training, and conditioning, to name a few. It is not advised to take on this kind of race if an individual's life is sedentary without the proper training and ample time to build discipline, momentum, and sustainable habits.

This would be the equivalent of going from Creeping straight to Running without spending time in the Crawling and Walking stages.

Taking on too much too soon is about establishing unrealistic or overly optimistic goals. Pace yourself.

Start with the end in mind and then develop the blueprint to get there. There can be long term implications for taking on too much too soon, such as the potential for injury or actions that could create mental or physical scars.

2. Failing to plan effectively

It can be said that the fulfillment of your goals is heavily based on the effectiveness of the overall plan.

Do you have a clearly defined goal with milestones?

Do you have a way to measure success? Do you know where the 'finish line' is located?

Do you have an idea of what it will cost to get started or sustain the goal?

There is a full system of steps that one can take to ensure proper planning takes place. Be sure to check out the book, "Roadmap to Success, Moving from the 95 who fail to the five who succeed" for the practical guide.

Having a system that can be used to measure progress helps to track success. By planning effectively and measuring success along the way, this allows one to monitor performance practically. It becomes more tangible, realistic, and obtainable.

Tracking progress keeps the goal on the top of your mind and minimizes distractions that are likely to occur.

3. Not having a precise measure of intentionality

Simply put, why is the fulfillment of your goal important? Having a clear understanding of intentional actions that are needed, being engaged, and having an emotional tie for why you want to fulfill the goal is essential.

Perseverance is necessary when obstacles threaten your commitment to the goal. Just because you do not hit the mark the first time does not mean that you should give up. It just means that you may need to re-adjust your approach, update your technique, try again, and continue to try.

In doing so, you are, in fact, developing your muscle memory. In doing this, it becomes more conceivable for you to multiply and replicate success in other areas of your life.

Be willing to have a pad and pen handy to ensure that you keep on the continuum of learning.

4. Wishing without work

Believing that you will reach your goal without doing any work does not get you closer to your goal, but it could take you farther away from it.

Lack of intentional focus in a particular direction lessens one's ability to achieve direct success. Therefore, it is important to do something every single day towards your goal. This can be to research, take trainings, walking, envisioning, planning, etc.

Every day as you do it, you begin to breathe life into it, and you begin to condition your mind for it.

Wishing it into existence leaves the fulfillment of your goal to happenstance. Rather than wait for it, make steps towards it.

5. Becoming distracted by Naysayers

It is important to keep in mind that many individuals may not believe in your goal or share the same drive towards it as you do. This is "OK."

Instead of getting distracted by this, find one or two people who do believe in your goal and can help you along the way.

Negativity can be contagious if it is not properly disposed of or displaced with positivity.

Trailblazers typically understand that a new idea is often rejected many times before it is accepted. This is true whenever setting a record occurs. Keep the optimism towards your goal and keep working on it.

6. Expecting Perfection on the first try

In the pursuit of your goals, recognize that you may not get it right the first time; however, making productive progress is the real measure.

Perseverance and perfection can only be built through gradual progression.

If you recall, perfection occurs only through repetition. Seek to grow as you go. Celebrate the incremental wins along the way.

Remember, your journey is just a step away; exercising wisdom will help to guide you and give you practical insights to making bold shifts where needed.

Steps to Leading with Your Feet

The process of getting into gear can be summed up into a few critical steps to ensure success.

First, recognize your goal. Envision it and **Give yourself a PUSH**... Knowing that you can do it and that you have everything you need in your immediate surroundings to get started should prompt action.

Next, **Get in Gear to Get It Done!** Execution requires action. Creating space right in the midst of what you have going on in life removes excuses while encouraging action.

Action is stimulated by the emotional connection that you have toward the goal, activating the process of movement, and having personal accountability. Ensure that you can tie the reason why you are striving for your goal back to a broader purpose or ambition. This occurs both internally and externally. The internal ensures that your goal gets done with your own personal resourcefulness, while the external connects it back to a larger vision and ensures that the goal is sustainable.

As part of Getting in Gear, you must move and develop momentum. Momentum, when it begins to build, can take down anything in its path.

Momentum is necessary.

It is the thing that keeps your goal fresh on your mind; it is with consistent movement that momentum is built.

If you are trying to get started on a vision, goal, or business and it just feels insurmountable in terms of understanding where to get started, it may be helpful to challenge yourself to **associate your goal with some other physical representation** of the goal (like a challenging race or walk).

Try investing in a race or tangible event that will help become the physical representation of the mental battles that you must overcome to pursue the goal. It is more difficult to conceive something in your mind and understand how to bring it into realization than it is to see physical steps taken by moving your feet.

When you start moving with your feet, you begin to feel and understand what it is like to get your body going. The same can be true as it relates to bringing your goals into view.

Sometimes it helps just to get a physical representation of the mental struggle so that you can execute physically, and as you work towards overcoming the physical (race or event of your choice), you begin to see ways to overcome the obstacles that keep you from obtaining your goals.

Just as if you were trying to work yourself into doing a half marathon, initially it may feel as though you cannot do it. As you begin to do it, you'll find that it is easier to have tangible results in overcoming your physical struggle because you are able to match results and have a tangible reflection of your goal. You can physically see your results materializing and happening. Establish milestones that are conceivable, achievable, and can be measured.

The next step is to **Give It Back or Give Ahead!** This notion connects your vision to a larger community and gives back to others who may want to follow that path that you have now created. In doing so, you begin to live vicariously through others.

The fourth step is to **Get out of the Pit** and recognize that there is no magic medicine that one can take to get there. Achieving your goals requires intentionality, preparation, desire, and dedication.

CLOSING

Leading with feet is an empowerment movement focused on invoking action to carry out legacy. There are a lot of battles that take place not just within the movement of your feet, but also conditioning of your mind. With every step taken, it is one step closer, even if you must take a step back.

Sometimes regression is necessary for progression...

Even if steps were missed or overlooked along the way.

Keep moving forward; keep moving forward!

The more you continue to activate momentum, the easier it becomes. The thing about momentum is once you begin, the laws of life begin to help propel you to where you need to go.

This process of building momentum, learning how to get your feet moving, and activating motion allows you to build resilience and helps you to manifest your dreams effectively.

On the opposite side of movement is stagnation. Most things that are not moving and do not continue to grow eventually stagnates and dies over time.

So, how bad do you want it? Or are you comfortable with where you are?

If you really want it, start moving. The beautiful thing about the human mind is the key aspect of muscle memory.

The more you do something, the more accustomed you become with doing it, and the easier it becomes.

Recognize that you cannot skip steps and go from Creeping to Running in the first try.

It is a process, and it would be beneficial to eliminate the mindset of believing that we can just go from the start of something to the finish without enduring the process of growth or rigor that comes along with it.

It is that process that allows you to be more prone, more perceptive, and ready for that next step.

What you will find is that if you intend to go from crawling to running without process, you will become underdeveloped in areas that are needed for flawless execution, and you can stall or eventually stop progress.

"Give careful thought to the paths for your feet and be steadfast in all your ways." - **Proverbs 4:26**

So, as we continue throughout this process of leading with feet, recognize that the feet are simply an analogy and symbolic for movement.

However, before movement can happen, and before you can accomplish anything in life, you must believe that you can. You must believe that you have to put your feet in motion to achieve anything. This process takes time, it takes patience, and it takes repetition to get back.

As you embark on this journey to lead with your feet, celebrate the small wins. As you celebrate those small wins, you are reinvigorating yourself and the belief that you can reach your goal. There is nothing like being able to push yourself and to continue to push yourself through it.

Recognizing that as you lead with your feet; it is not a straight path, it oscillates, it is sometimes isolated, and is more like a tangled string.

Sometimes you go backward, forward, up, down, or even left and right. The point is that you continue to progress and move because, with every detangle and with every curve, you learn. Learning is exactly what you want to do. It is the only way that you train and get better. It is the only way that you perfect your craft and get better with striving, driving, and thriving.

So, get moving! The world awaits your unique greatness.

Sue found herself back in Singapore exactly seven years later. There she stood at the security terminal, her silk pink and white top sat just above her neatly pleated white skirt. She took a breath and exhaled a chuckle as she smiled while grabbing her bag off the belt.

She could not believe that the last time she walked this airport, she was distraught and in a state of disarray. Sue shook her head, recalling that day. She took the same walk through the terminal, this time with a smile.

She stopped in the restroom and closed her eyes, reflecting on the sound of her sobs that once filled the space. She walked over to the stall where she once cried and pushed the door slightly open while gazing in. 'Wow, I remember this exact stall,' she whispered aloud. She turned and left the restroom.

As if she were picking up breadcrumbs that outlined the walk she took previously; she reimagined her journey. This time she thought about the years that separated her last walk in the airport, and how so much in her life changed. She had grown so much. With a slight smirk on her face, she shook her head while taking a stroll through memory lane.

A few moments later, she began to slow her pace, and her heart began to race. To the left of her was the bookstore that spoke to her. She peered in. As if her feet were frozen in place, she stood at the entry and gazed inside. There it was, the gorgeous book display case, the one that gave her a glimmer of hope the last time she saw it. The case still stood next to a display that read the words" Best Seller." Only this time, there were books on the table.

She became overwhelmed with gratitude, and the tears began to well once more in her eyes. This time, they were tears of joy.

Finally, Sue made her way into the store.

She stopped at the display case, and through watery eyes, picked up the book, **her book**. She smiled, remembering the day she felt dismal, wishing she had inspiration in a time that she was in disarray.

That day, she resolved that she would write and share her journey in hopes that it would help other people. So, she did. She wrote it, and she shared it. Who knew, seven years later, it would be featured as a best seller in the very bookstore that gave her the inspiration.

"Ms. Sue," she heard a voice from the back of the store. Sue turned to see the store attendant patiently waiting to address her.

"Oh, hi, yes!" She called back to her while blinking away her tears and moving towards the attendant.

"We are so excited to host your book signing," the attendant eagerly shook Sue's hand.

"You have no idea, what it means to me," Sue replied with a chuckle.

"Right this way, and we will get you set up," the attendee said while guiding Sue to the back of the store.

She clung to her book and smiled. Sue lowered her gaze in humble appreciation as she disappeared behind the store door.

Your next chapter awaits you!

Peace and blessings!

Charelle Lans

REFERENCES

1. Les Brown, Goodreads.com-
   https://www.goodreads.com/quotes/
   884712-the-graveyard-is-the-richest-
   place-on-earth-because-it

2. Webster's Dictionary-
   https://www.merriam-
   webster.com/dictionary/fear

3. World-Statistics.org http://world-
   statistics.org/

4. Tony Robbins:
   https://www.facebook.com/TonyRob
   bins/posts/10151092879379060

5. Mason, John. *An Enemy Called
   Average*, Naperville, Illinois: Simple
   Truths 2011, Print.

6. The Bible: KJV, James 2:20

7. Bill Bradley, Biography.com,
   https://www.biography.com/people/
   bill-bradley-9223478

8. Mason, John. *An Enemy Called Average,* Naperville, Illinois: Simple Truths 2011, Print.

9. Twitter, Dave Ramsey Show @Ramseyshow #DaveDaily; https://twitter.com/RamseyShow/status/366935638622220290

10. Steve Ferrante, Pinnacle Performance Champions, https://pinnacleperformancechampions.org/tag/sales-success/

11. Mason, John. *An Enemy Called Average,* Naperville, Illinois: Simple Truths 2011, Print.

12. Steve Mehr; http://thedailyquotes.com/child-learns-walk/

13. Bible NIV, Proverbs 4:26 http://www.biblica.com/bible/niv/proverbs/4/

14. www.goodreads.com https://www.goodreads.com/author/quotes/879.Plato

15. Hal Elrod, Hal Elrod International http://halelrod.com/hal-elrods-top-10-inspirational-empowering-quotes/

16. Ralph Waldo Emerson, Wikiquote.org https://simple.wikiquote.org/wiki/Ralph_Waldo_Emerson

ABOUT THE AUTHOR

Charelle Lans is an award-winning author, vision strategist, Industrial Engineer, Engagement & Motivational Speaker, Development Coach, and Executive who believes in cultivating "Loved Limitless Leaders."

She is an engaging motivational speaker and accomplished professional with a passion for driving people and process performance to enable their highest productivity while yielding greater profitability.

She is the President and Lead Strategist for Vision Strategy Management, LLC., and active in many organizations.

BACKGROUND:

Charelle has authored the three-time award-winning book, "Leading with Feet," *Making Intentional Steps to Live Out Your Best" first edition.* This international book has had sellout signings internationally and has been impacting lives on a global scale.

"Leading with Feet" is an inspirational book that focuses on inspiring action to create movement. Charelle has been featured in various publications.

Through her powerful and life-changing speeches and training, she has touched the lives of numerous individuals, including Fortune 500 companies.

Originally from Miami, Florida, Charelle has been most notably called by many who encounter her as a 'woman beyond her years.'

Charelle never let circumstance hinder her drive to defy the odds, whether it was attending a school **over two hours away** or **saving millions** for Fortune 500 companies.

Charelle has carved her path to becoming an engaged, energetic, and strategic business executive who believes 'when people live their best, they can **give** their best.

With **over ten years of industry experience**, she has and continues to do just that! She has served on a number of boards working to increase the presence of Women & Minority in leadership and STEM roles.

She volunteers her time working to mentor, teach, and coach women and minorities in the areas of personal leadership and strategic/business planning aimed at helping individuals and businesses to develop sustainable strategic success through a foundational copywritten approach. She works to create generational legacy minded thought leaders.

Made in the USA
Columbia, SC
27 November 2024